As Girls Could Boast

First published in 1994 by The Oscars Press,
BM Oscars, London WC1X 3XX.
Reprinted 1995.
Poems copyright © individual authors 1994.
This anthology © Christina Dunhill 1994.
Introduction copyright © Christina Dunhill 1994.

ISBN 1-872668-03-8
British Library Cataloguing-in-Publication Data: A catalogue record
for this book is available from the British Library.

**LONDON
ARTS BOARD**

Financially assisted by the London Arts Board.

Distributed by Turnaround, 27 Horsell Road, London N5 1XL (UK).
Inland Book Co, PO Box 120261, 140 Commerce Street, East Haven,
CT 06512 (USA).

The Oscars Press is a member of the Association of Little Presses and the
Small Press Group of Britain.

Typesetting by Counter Productions, London.
Printed and bound in England by Biddles of Guildford.

As Girls Could Boast

new poetry by women

Edited by Christina Dunhill

The Oscars Press

For Wendy

ACKNOWLEDGEMENTS

Title from Emily Dickinson's poem Nº 299 in *Collected Poems* (Faber, 1970).

Previous publication of poems as follows:

'Corinna Revisited' in *Spokes*, Winter 1993;
'Zebra Zebra' in *Poetry London Newsletter,* vol 4, no.1;
'Sweet peas flowering unexpectedly' in *The Rialto*, Summer 1991;
'Counting' in the *Sunday Times* Books section, March 13, 1994 ;
'Memento' in *The Cutting Room*;
'Raw' in *Raw* (Wide Skirt Press) and in *The Sycamore Review*, Purdue University, Indiana;
'Friday Night' in the *Siddur* (prayerbook) of Beit Klal Yisrael;
'Steeplechase Park' in *Five Women Poets* (Crocus Press);
'Houdini' in *Poetry Review* New Generation Poets issue, 1994;
'Eisriesenwelt' in the *South West Poetry Anthology*, 1993;
'Teeth' in *The Observer*, 1993.

My thanks to all the contributors, extra thanks to Moniza Alvi, Pascale Petit and Ruth Valentine. Thanks also to fellow Oscars, Steve Anthony and Peter Daniels.

CONTENTS

4 *Courtship Dance*

5 *Angel Wrestling*

6 *Gravity*

7 *Burnt Notebook*

8 *Less and Less*

INTRODUCTION

This is a collection of bold and individual poems, a collection of women's poems. It is representative only of a kind of energy: the energy of telling it like it is. This energy embraces all emotion and thought, from the rhapsodic to the vituperative; its only demand is that its form be found for it, it be made flesh.

The original idea on which these poems were solicited was risk — for the hell of it, and thinking of writing out of the body, out of emotion, vision and actual poetic risk, the risk we all take when we do it — moving between the force for meaning and the potential for chaos. And they were solicited on the anthology's title.

Of course, poems are shy things, not often suited to attitude and flaunting. They glimmer by in the half light, winking at you under a 40 watt bulb; irresolution and ambiguity are the stuff of them. They throw themselves away with a twist or a joke, a waggle of their butt as they pass you. Perhaps it is the tension between this truth and the rival ideas of boast and risk which gives this collection its identity.

So how have these ideas transmuted? The boast seems to have become the poem itself, or language, and the risk what we can make it carry. The practice of poetry seems central here, there are the conceits that we are ourselves written by or written on by experience, and equally that we are part of a universe wanting to write itself through us. A face transmits *its urgent wish to meet itself on paper*[1]. In this way the boast is our offering to the world, and our belonging. And there seems to be a seeking of grace, of restoration to the animal and natural world we have fallen from; through that very language which signifies our difference we appease and seek re-entry. Or we may seek the *flesh-language*[2] as if we might tap into some undifferentiated and all-consoling love. But equally we seek it to celebrate the loves we've got: *Do not be afraid, Sweet Heart. / This is not a spelling test, it is a kiss*[3]. We turn on men the gaze we've been gazed by. We turn it on women. We turn it on the gods (*She came to me / in a dream of enormous bosoms*[4]). We speak in voices and inhabit other forms.

All the risk in the world will be bombast if the poem can't hold it. There are poems here about gruelling events lifted by the quality of observation, poems driven by spluttering outrage carried by liturgical attention to detail — *I was born into Hell. / In May the central heating's still on as well as / the Cosy Glo*[5] — fantastical revenges such as Selima Hill's. Ruth Valentine's fine unblinking *Burnt Notebook* is both invocation and exorcism.

People talk of flights of fancy but imagination is also a horse we need to ride. *He touches my insides as though / he'd sighted the first landplants*[6] or:

He kept me in his belly
three days and threw me up at Nineveh,
expecting me to do the business. Which I did,
knowing by then that angels need respect
as well as wrestling. As do whales.[7]

How can we digest the indigestible? What do we do with the bitter pill we've swallowed? Pascale Petit literally builds the world of her childhood and the giant icedolls speak back: *Welcome to our sitting-room. / It's hard to cross it, so we don't.*[8] Jackie Kay on the boy watching the police killing of Joy Gardner: *He will watch her hands smash and thrash. / His hands making a church, then a tall / steeple. He crosses his fingers. Squeezes them. / His hands wet themselves.*[9] Killings in war and peace are in focus, as is death and our fear of it. The collection ends with a pietà section:

death has scooped you
out of me
broken the cradle
of your arms
exiled you to the abominable
mantelpiece of candlesticks [10]

I have grouped the sections as lightly as I could. The aim was to put in white space as we do in a poem, to drop air in, as much as to divide. The sections are a means of juggling, a way of linking and separating while suspending, for example, the erotic, the plaintive, the exquisite, the visionary, the outrageous, the terrifying, the bizarre.

Christina Dunhill
June 1994

1. Mimi Khalvati.
2. Carol Rumens
3. Penelope Shuttle.
4. Gwyneth Lewis.
5. Judy Gahagan.
6. Moniza Alvi.
7. Julia Casterton.
8. Pascale Petit.
9. Jackie Kay.
10. Alison Fell.

Everything is Possible

Animals

Speak to me in a language where every word
ends with an O and the hood goes down
on my understanding. Make me ignorant.
I don't want to know what you are saying
only the sounds you make. And I don't want
to be human, but a cat, perhaps a cat
who has waited for just your voice and
the language of your hands. Speak to me in
code, as you would to a gorilla mute with
grief. As you would speak to animals,
softly, knowing you can ease them not with
words but with the meaning of the music
under words. Let your tongue be foolish
on me. Let me cleave to the roof of your mouth.

Julia Casterton

Sweet Heart

Here I am, Sweet Heart, my long white Lizzie Siddal skirts
rustling in wonder,
and my pretty yet stoic black-lace bustier...

Do not be afraid, Sweet Heart.
This is not a spelling test, it is a kiss,

truly, and a way for us to become just like other people,
tall and kingly and happy,
drifting together every night in a cloud of sweet indecent
 smells...

It is for you I make lewd guesses.
It is for you, Sweet Heart, I carry the sky on my back.
It is for you I eat large meals, to become strong.

It is for you I sing amid my eternal furniture.
But I sing in such a way that no one is upset,
for it suggests merely the gifted amateur.

Do not be afraid.

Did you know I have a favourite ocean?
Look down, Sweet Heart,
into its deep tarnish-green waters. See angel-swoop
of passing shark, there;
how he glides away in smiling narrow-minded self-absorption?
Who is afraid?

Penelope Shuttle

Angel Falls in Love

Nobody had seen a waterfall so high. He thought
I was the last thing people see when they die.

His plane rose vertically until it reached the dot
my three-thousand-foot fall pours out of.
Then he crash-landed on my mountain
and called it Devil's Mountain.

He stood over me and shouted his name — Angel,
Jimmy Angel. I think he married me because
he gave me his name. All I'd known was this
hot stone that rises out of the clouds into thin air.
His eyes were blue as this sky. In them I saw myself,

two selves in his sunglasses. He kissed me.
He leant over the precipice and drenched his face,
couldn't get close enough. He must have been wondering
how the hell he could escape, back to his kind.

Since then, there's been the rare visitor.
Once a film crew appeared to make *The Lost World*
and I swayed, I danced for them, I roared, I sang,
making my debut to the rest of the earth.
then they left, and there was this silence.

Pascale Petit

Corinna Revisited

So you returned, Naso. My door is not
that securely locked and before I knew it
you'd ivied in. The hottest time of day:
a small sun trembled against the flawless sky
like beaded sweat on skin, and one closed
shutter dredged half the room with cloud.
Sandals lip-smacked across the tiles: Wake
up. He's back - that poet; Wake up, he's back —
That poet, you, appeared, eyes as wide
as The Tiber and so deep I could have dived
in and drowned. They swallowed up the scene,
every feature sprawling along the horizon,
and in seconds you'd scanned pastures, peaks,
chasms - the enormous prospect of sex
unfolding before you over the couch. Your choice
was deep South, that short-shadowed place
steeped in topography. You set out
from there, pacing yourself in its sour heat,
breaking words out of the air, seeds
of lines falling into the sheet's folds.
You made great strides with me that afternoon,
until evening set the town's lights gasping
and the thin street-trees froze to smoke.
By then even our sharp contours were slack.
As for inspiration, I'd had a belly
full, and you'd enough hips, thighs,
breasts and lips for a twelve-part volume
on anatomy. So I said, 'Lover, time
you went home,' and pointed at a grey ridge
of clothes stretching the length of my Indian rug.
The toughest climb today: you lifting up
your tired head's weight from my lap.
It rose slowly. 'One thing more, Naso,'
(as you fastened your belt). 'Before you go
and let all this loose on paper, look —
my poem, finished, thanks to your hard work.'

Christina Moran

15

Tara's Visit

She came to me
in a dream of enormous bosoms,
magnificent lallers,
not hers but mine,
that had grown from nothing,
ripened and swelled
till they overflowed my office blouse
and were... a phenomenon.
My colleagues looked on
but no one was rude
about my stupendous amplitude.

Word spread and other workers came
to see for themselves
so I fed them,
telling them all the while
of how it is that all is well
and how endlessly
the miracle welled up in me
of her kindness and generosity.

And then the hall
was filled with my hair
and knowing this
was really her
we swam in the whorls
of her fragrant care

and nobody minded
no work was done
for Tara held us
in her plenitude,
for her help is warm,
her breath is food!

Gwyneth Lewis

Tara is a Buddhist deity, especially helpful in overcoming difficulties.

Everything is Possible

I want you to know
that if I really wanted to
I could jump off this Royal Albert Hall
balcony
in the middle of the concert
and swing on a floating fungal acoustic device
bellowing like a gorilla
right into that vasty chasm
blooming over everyone's heads.
Every time I come here
I think about doing it,
it sends the thrills
shooting up my legs.
Fortunately
the fear of heights
a desire to avoid social ridicule
and a reluctance to interrupt the music
have prevented me
up to now.

Cate Parish

Zebra Zebra

A zebra lies out on the flatlands
in extremis, tinctured.
It has swum in a storm.
All its head is pulled back as if listening.
The ink steals into its ears.

Three lion cubs find the zebra.
Their shirt-tails are out.
They have come through the long grass
tussling, tumbling
past the heartbeat of their mother.

The sun dumps its white-blue over the path.
The cubs walk over the zebra's india ink,
their good fortune, jump its legs,
hesitate on the brink. The zebra's
breath has gone back to the plain, the pollen.

They do not yet know
how to tear and devour
but the zebra is surprising
as a child sees henna at a wedding
on a hand, a foot,

or the river leaves behind
its fiery pattern in the silt,
the story of how it bore away
the naked fish. I lifted my book of poems
from the deep box one Christmas.

I was lame with a piece of glass in my foot.
I took the Songs of Innocence
and Experience into the kitchen,
away from the other children.
How slyly the words were chosen

you could whisper them —
those dazzling lines drawn painstakingly
across a life, like losses.

Jane   Duran

The Face

Apart from — under the line of the eyebrow —
a line of olive swelling as an olive swells
to a glint of cream, two round black eyes
like two black cherries and those two plucked lines

surprised to find themselves so high above her eyes
no dialogue takes place
in all that space left in between

nothing, as you pass her in the street,
of her face remains

except a certain light, a clarity,
a reflection not of sun or cloud
but of an image of desire,

an image of becoming
she has placed like God in sky
and though she thinks it private, preceding her
like sun, like cloud, clear to any passerby

it pours across her face, unwritten, bare,
the force of all those futures
we have in mind, we had in mind
and some we failed and some we now embody:

not an inner light, not an outer
though the sky glares and her face
is turned towards the place the sun should be

19

(and yours towards the station
with the light behind your back where motorways
span farmland, ring roads, open country)

but on her skin, an emptiness that glows
the way an empty morning
clarifies to an urgency, an image

whose name or face you do not know
but feel its tug, its urgent wish
to meet itself on paper
and by being seen, by seeing warn

the emptiness so filled with light, dream, hope
it cannot know
the worlds between

the beacon and the lines
that will get written
as they did on mine
on a face that passes in the street.

Mimi Khalvati

Pan

Since I was ill-wished
by the priests, my kisses
are no more
than a pin-up's red, insipid
gesture of the mouth.

Beware of him, they said.
You'll know
at once, by his ice-cold dick,
their own
kept in a strict order.
By then, I thought, surely
it will be too late.
But where was my lip to say so?

Besides, here I am, rigid
and cold as a speculum,
searching for bad cells.
Relax, I say, smiling, relax,
if you don't it will hurt.

Sometimes, on wet pavements
under the blue
ring of a street-lamp, I meet
a woman who finds me attractive.
But I can make do with the most
stiff-necked of votaries.
I stand my ground.
Warm me, I command,
warm me.

Rosemary Norman

The Wasps

Our mother liked to feed me perfect veal;
and 2 invisible drops of *Radiostol*
were wobbled on my morning toast by Nurse
— a special little wafer, like a host.
She fed my upstairs sister next to nothing.
At least, that's what my upstairs sister thought.
And when I tried to move her head, I couldn't.
And when her kitten started licking her,
bit by bit, as if she were a skyscraper
a tiny *Tippex* brush was painting white,
I ran into the yard to greet the wasps,
and let the licking carry on all night
— my sister on her bed, and me outside,
my naked body smeared with marmalade.

Selima Hill

The Purr

The Purr

When the boy knew he would never be listened to,
He fell asleep. This photograph confirms it:
Sleep in the boy's hand, reaching absent-hearted
To smoothe the equable forehead of *Morsilka*
Sleep in the purr we hear from her tabby frown,
Her barrelled rump, the powder-puffs of her haunches:
Sleep in the stern, near-masculine little profile
That denies itself a study, though the father
Shouts *Keep Still,* and the glass eye glares: that denies
It could ever meet desire in a woman's look.
Morsilka, the boy's slyly parted lips
Are saying in cat-talk: *Morr, Morr, Morsilka.*

Dormancy's always attractive in a man
— Ask the rise-and-shine brigade of his admirers.
When he was 25, they'd have cut their names
In his skin to see the colour of his eyes
— Too late, by a hundred years!
He slept and slept, heavy as the Ukraine
In Europe's gut, as vodka on the liver,
Woke to father a child or two, fell away
To deeper sleep, his electrician's hands
Curling into their knowledgeable darkness.
Now when I pause, last naked straggler, coldly
Equable in the beam of his sleeping vision
I deem it a privilege not to be roughly parted,
And thrown on like a favourite dressing-gown,
But wear my own hand, guiltlessly and lightly,
And murmur self-talk: *Morr, Morr, Morsilka.*

Because my foam will never trouble him,
I leave it on his lips, free of charge.
Because it speaks my favourite language, silence,
I make sleep-love to his carved and studious back.
His rest and my retreat are perfect partners
Like boy and cat. Or, like a woman, found
By the only woman, when the long notes drawn
At length from one another's sleeping fur
Call back the dawn before we fell asleep
To bear the breaking day, that utterly clear
Wakefulness. *Morsilka*, our smiles say
Might be the first word of a flesh-language
We always knew but only now have tasted
In the strong original: *Morr, Morr, Morsilka*.

Note: Morr, morr *is what Russian cats say instead of purr, purr. The infinitive of the verb is* Morlikat.

Carol Rumens

Starlet

Six feet under I am flying high,
a saint to artful women.
The tabloids chart my upward rise
beyond the likes of page three girls
and readers' wives. The secret?
Girls, steal a tip from Marlene Dietrich,
who had ten-millimetre pearls
sewn into all her evening dresses
to make her nipples larger than life.

Or Jean Harlow, who dyed her pubic hair
platinum, wore only silver satin,
drove a man to suicide on their wedding night,
and died herself soon after (that's important,
girls, don't outstay your welcome).
Jayne Mansfield went out
with a bang, all along the highway,
took her poodle with her,
now how's that for a grand finale?

Me? I went peacefully in my sleep
aided by gin and valium,
still young enough to have avoided the knife,
or the Greta Garbo recluse routine.
I expect to be an angel now, in some kind
of chiffon number and a halo, get the picture?
But girls, I can see you down there,
dancing around your handbags
and marrying the first asshole who asks.

I can tell you now there's nothing romantic
in the stars, balls of gas and rock
and dust. You can see through everything
if you look hard enough; illusion
is what makes it beautiful.
Develop your mystery, girls, after
innocence, it's all you have left.
Or make something up. Where I am now,
they'll never know the difference.

Tamar Yoseloff

When The Lights Go Up

You promise a beginning, like the smooth
opening of the long, dark drapes
in the cinema, which whisper
'I will take all your pain away'.

When I hear your red Rover
change into third at the bottom of our hill
it seems to growl like the MGM lion
'I will make you insatiable'.

You laugh when I haven't been funny,
your laugh, smoky as Talisker,
and feed me salted popcorn
glazed with butter and gunpowder.
Your eyes burn and flicker,
'I will show you a good time'.

You bathe me in rosemary
wrap me in a thick blanket of new skin
and call softly from a black and white film
'You are the most beautiful thing
I have ever seen'.

I could almost feel the ground slip
your palm settle on my brow,
taste your melted chocolate
almost eat your baked vanilla buns
believe you when you say
'Believe me'.
But when the phone rings after midnight
I let it ring.

Cherry Smyth

Body Copy

after Montaigne's essay on clothes

These are the jeans. Everyone wears them.
They button up the front. They have loops for a belt.
Fuck the jeans. It's your legs I want
wrapped around me
rocking back.

And this is a good haircut.
Fourteen pounds. Makes a man stand out.
Let that go. I'd want you as Nebuchadnezzar,
hair and nails rooting earth.

This T shirt now, it's white.
It says Bonjour at the neck.
Take the damn thing off.

I want your body *sans* an advertising break
in a room that's warm enough.
Now undress.
Let me see you as a naked man,
all face.

Julia Casterton

Just

I know what I want. I want
you to walk down Marylebone
Road with no clothes on. Not
in the t-shirt for sale in
the shop by the Planetarium, black
with inane print on, but just
you, bare. Not stopping the traffic
but walking uninterrupted on
the cans and spit. London dirt
collecting around the soft skin
of your toes, your pale parts
looking pale in the pavement
light. And I try to imagine:
the look on your face; what
you would do with your arms
(swing them, nonchalant?)
and your hands (cup them
around your balls? both or each
in turn?); women going past
without even a backward glance.
You would be unremarked on
but remarked by me. I want
this just as I have been in
mind in your places without
much on. Say, an enamel bath,
raising my leg to soap my skin,
rubbing gently between my toes.

Christina Moran

Sweet Peas Flowering Unexpectedly

The sweet peas startled me, with labial flowers,
curves and folds in all the right places —
different shades of red and lilac, mauve and blue
and deep, rich, shocking pink, still holding dew.

Here is a sweet pea, unexpected in my garden
(I never planted it — it turned up, pink, last summer)
here is a sweet pea. All of a sudden
I want to run my fingers round it,
stick my tongue inside it, lick it,
go out secretly, eating sweet peas at night
creating local shortages
and scandals in local gardens,
raiding flower shows, munching bunches,
a floral sex maniac
hooked on erotic encounters,
mouth to petal.

Today I caused a stir in the garden centre;
I bought two thousand, five hundred sweet pea seeds.
The back garden has a tall fence, now;
I've dug up the lawn.
I will sow sweet peas by moonlight,
every one of them;
feasting next summer demented and ecstatic
entwined in flowers and dew in my sweet pea bed.

Jan Sellers

Counting the Ways

The way your tongue tracks
a sticky snail's path down, a parting
of lips, a musky kiss; the way

you take chocolate, whisky, breath
from my mouth, swallow them as you would me,
you say, then demonstrate how you kiss

your wife, the wife who trims the grey
at your temples; the way your face shows
all its years, crumpled in orgasm;

the way you dry me from the shower,
accompany the crassest lyrics, and believe
in them, inventory the whiteness

of my teeth, the mobility of my lips, the lie
of my cunt. You would buy me at auction,
you say. She says the paintwork needs washing,

the garden needs seeing to, the kids
need amusing, need a father, need more clothes.

Sue Rose

The Minotaur's Complaint

To Ariadne June's ambivalent, cloud-
stricken, a war between Saturn

and Mars. The sun blares omens
the earth ripples, volcanic.

In the mud of the labyrinth I trample
and sulk. Don't forget

it was Pasiphae who begat me
by a bull-god, guilty

and grunting in that wooden womb.
And now Ariadne's out

to get me, wringing her missionary
hands and slandering: that

white sister, she who crawls up
the virgin sheets, electric,

baring her scent
to the black muzzle of the night.

Like mother like daughter.
Afternoons under the tamarisk trees

the shadow-bull battles
in their swooning sleep.

Bent to the morning's baking
with the sea a blue hum

at the window, they rise
to him like yeast,

scandalous, their faces turned
from each other.

Ariadne hoards her prim
shame like honey. When she feasts

on her night fingers, who
is to blame but her brother

the beast, this sticky hybrid
in his sweltering hide.

Pay attention to Ariadne. See
how she plots in the nettle-

beds, hears the rumble of hooves
in the maze of her belly:

the quake, the stars
shaken loose.

See how she snorts now
at the red entrance

where her horns are, her flared
lips like nostrils, and the nip

of the gold ring that Theseus
might tug and tug.

Alison Fell

The Institute Ladies

Please Do Not Change In The Toilets
Please do not boss me about
like this. Please provide
at least some of the following:
bumph, mirror, hot water and
a towel. In return
I will try not to change
from mild to menacing.

Please Do Not Change In The Toilets
What — not change from
needy to relieved,
constipated to productive,
from scruffy to neat?
I've spent my life
learning to be regular:
what's a loo for?

Please Do Not Change In The Toilets
Too late. I have.
I walked in and caught her
combing her hair,
and I started
to run hot.

Rosanna Hibbert

A Sun and a Moon

Counting

Susan wants to attach scythes to the wheels
of her father's car and cut everyone off at the knees,
like Boadicea. She could flatten a town centre
as quickly as a combine harvester. She's referee
when I fight with Donna over a ruler; snapped,
beating a cage of locusts so they would try to escape.
As we smash each other against lockers, Susan counts.

Every thud on metal is a point. Outside the art room
she throttles me for losing and my throat stings with vomit
as an indigested pea is forced from my nostril.
When I jump on her head in the swimming pool
her gushing nose leaves a trail on the white tiles like steak
dripping inside our fridge. But we make peace in needlework,
sewing skirts short enough to be cut from remnants.

They will flap against our buttocks like shirt-tails
when we meet on Saturday in the Army and Navy cafe,
wrists smudged with lipstick — Fuchsia, Pink Passion,
Carnival, Hot Date. We put them on in the toilet mirror,
practising open-mouthed kisses on folded tissues —
the fine lines of our lips printed like the claws
of hungry birds treading lightly over snow.

Jackie Wills

2

When the sky showed both a sun and a moon
I went off with the twins. *Come home with us,*
they'd said to me, alone in the street
with my skipping rope, bells in the handles.

One twin skipped ahead, chiming and tinkling,
the other walked beside me, too close, close enough
for her sugary breath to tickle my cheek. The gardens
lengthened and deepened. They led me away;

smiling at the same time, making me
eat pink words on identical lovehearts. *Hi Chum.*
There was something odd that drew the eye
to their socks. Only their ribbons differed.

In here. When we got to their house
I was scared. Their four eager narrow eyes. Then
both of them swore, pulling me, as I sobbed, to
their wooden blue gate, its small white 2.

When I slipped, the gravel bit at my knees,
peppery. *There's two of us.* And when I ran
they chased me, yanking me back by the hair;
and what they did to me then they did to me twice.

Carol Ann Duffy

The Birds

It seems there wasn't any pain; you've come awake.
Wipe that blood from your face, he says —
perhaps the trees have grazed you.

He hands your bag across. It's made of cloth. Feel
first. Your face comes down and hits you,
sticky, bigger than it should be.

Part of you has hopped clean out of your head
and sits in the bush like a chaffinch
bars of blue behind the eyes:

      Hallo from my nest of hair,
      my little tea of beechmast,
      admire my breast, a sunburst.

Time's gone by and you weren't in it. Look down.
Something rolls over and thuds inside your head.
All your clothes are on.

But hard. Your jacket's stiff enough to walk away.
You're inside out. You're not who you were.
You're something alive in a butcher's shop.

Scream. You'd never heard yourself. In dreams
they don't come out. He had to keep on hitting you
until you stopped.

      Hallo little bouncing sparrow,
      lusty, dusty flutterbath, want some insects
      just take mine; want my house, I'll give it you.

'You're a nice girl,' he says slowly. 'I don't want
to hurt you — ,' You think this means he'll let you go.
He's going to say he's sorry.

      The birds will visit you again
      plop from chimney onto mat,

shake off the soot, then, white as nets —
stick out their small stiff tongues.

Christina Dunhill

Roses

A man
is selling roses

Single buds
roses for lovers
passionate and red.

He goes
from table to table
but the couples
all politely
shake their heads

and then, the man
selling roses
goes away
without asking
if I would like one too

because, after all
a woman would never
buy a rose just
for herself.

That night
I dream of roses
stretching out
into the distance

Not neat, cultivated beds
for people with
too much money

These are tangled clumps
that trail across pathways
making it impossible
to walk without falling
flat on your face.

My roses snatch
at your ankles and send
spiteful tendrils up
to entwine your heart.

My roses pull you down
and rub your nose
in the mud.

Dragged by thorns
and jagged leaves
I clamber through them
searching for the best place
to lie down.

Emma Greengrass

Your Nakedness

for my mother

your nakedness surprises us both
I've walked into your room
without knocking
just as I used to do
stop   seeing your nakedness
standing there between us

as surprised as we are
for a moment
standing perfectly still
like a doe startled
by the rustle of footsteps
inside the quiet of her forest

then darting suddenly for cover
in small sharp bounds
your nakedness is gone
as flustered
you turn your back to me
your hands rushing to pick up
the blue nylon slip
you've worn under your dresses
ever since I can remember

don't look don't look at me
you say holding the material
pressed close against you

standing in front of you
I feel awkward and clumsy
as though I'd frightened away
the youngest and most tender part of you
and yet it's your old age
you're trying to hide
wrinkles and soft flesh
and the scar which grows
where your left breast should be
the scar I never saw
only imagined
pain you thought
you could hide from me
all these years
holding it pressed against yourself

Maria Jastrzebska

Memento

In the place where the islanders
obey the speed limit,
where garage becomes hairdresser
becomes post office becomes store,
where the farmer's wife invites me for tea
in the house where the farmer was born,
you can't get more shiftless than that,
I have left a pair of shorts in the drawer,
I have left a pair of mint green silk shorts
in the second drawer down in the chest.

Where fulmars glide like balsa wood planes
over patches of glisten on the sea,
larks still their song over quilted hills,
buttercup, double poppy, moist green,
where the land is indented with water,
cows with pierced ears paddle lochs
or reply to the wails of the seals
on farms fenced down to the shore.

Where dawn is intimate with dusk,
a place called Wilderness impossible to find,
where the farmers offer me drop scones
and three kinds of cake, where they once
lived in the cottage next door, newly wed,
where their son will live with his wife,
I have left silk shorts in the drawer
of the farmers who are afraid of large towns,
in the place where I am afraid of the cows.

Chrissie Gittins

Your preference, you say, is to make love in the afternoon

that light outside ensure the dark baptism be brief,
the furniture you inherit gleam essential, and discreet
love, managed, have its place in this monumental city:
timed fascination, trial separation, anguish scripted
extinguish joy. Replace with calm satisfaction compassed!
I hear the manly purr of engines not anthems to the sunset.

I'm unmanageable as a tall horse with a terrified eye
you can't quieten, only sea at night would quieten me,
or even worse, managed, I turn to stone, a monument
to a long lost cause, disconsolate on a plinth,
the fanning mocking sweet doves of love encircle.
Why must I by-pass my heart? Oh bruised fruit!

In your house love's kept in its black plush box
in a drawer behind the intricate family games, locked up.
I'd thought it was something written, a figment
in a book, high on a shelf, not opened in years.
At the door to your house you puff your importance up,
cold adder. I stroke my schwärmerei. Measly little cat!

Where would I make love then? My penniless love-death?
My Orpheic shadowing? It would be night, not afternoon:
the room dark and soft as Christmas; a place low down
and very close to trees, to animals curious and quiet;
my love would be an oblivion. I know of no etiquette
for rising unscathed groomed into your normalized light.

Judy Gahagan

Training Scheme

Words fall in the classroom, strange fruits.
and I'm the outsider, close, yet apart
gulping at familiar bitter seeds, 'Poll-tax... benefits...'
envying the bilingual, I stare at codes....

Bengali is half-moon hieroglyphics;
scrolls mirrored and unravelling underwater,

مو اسم حجرہ اتی

the Urdu for 'My house is cold,' kites and butterflies,
scarves drifting in an easterly wind;
the emblems of the Gujerat, embroidered stitches
on a sleeve. This one, perhaps, blue silk,
threads coming loose and a hole punched through.
'Is this fault recoverable?'
Your smiles rippling in complicity prove
how well you know this game and so
we pool fluencies and the raw imperfections
of my official tongue dissolve.
(Language to survive by when your house is cold
and the burglars have been and scavenged in the night.)

Now swapping photos we touch the shapes
which form each other's lives.
This boy, with hair like corn,
a little girl with kohl-black eyes.
Childhoods unplundered.
Nimisha laughs, the sun shifts clouds,
her belly a hard bud at seven months' gone,
remembers when she walked to school at dawn,
when prosperity was a field of grain
and a river, made legendary with flowers,
shone silver under a swollen moon. The best days....

Grey light inside this toy-box factory
exposes flaws; snags of gold,
spoilt blue material swathed like an unwound sea,
faults for you, me and our children,
stitching and unpicking dreams

and signing our names while the treadle effaces
our histories, calling to each other across
the river's stinking maw, disclaiming translations;
dumb sentences mouthed behind a veil.

Pam Thompson

Jesus loves me, this I know

because the Bible
tells me so
I have old school assembly
hymns wrapped at the edge
of my tongue
I hear you
asking me
where the pain, the vein,
the drip, the bed clip
and I answer in
ba ba black sheep
have you
any wool rhymes
it's here in my skin,
my eyelashes,
my heart,
my lips,
my palms,
my brain it's in my
ding dong merrily
on high
from the painkillers
replacing the
high from the pain
the high from the thought
of finally going
the high places
I have to go
so I can leave

Maya Chowdhry

45

This is what it is like now

Now I no longer have the half minute on waking when you are not here.
Sleep soaked you up, there were thirty seconds in each day
when I was alone. I felt all the liberty of not having you inside me
just at the moment when you opened the door and barged back in.
Now not even that. In dreams I stretch out my arms and behind me
at my fingers' ends are your lips kissing them as they open backwards
to the light. I hold you as a baby, as a boy and as you are,
a young man under the water of his life. Only as an old man
have I not held you because when you are old I shall have gone
already and so there is no place for that dream in my dream.

Julia   Casterton

Courtship Dance

The Mind I Lose

Whether the things I feel are true
Or just illusion on my part
I think that I'm in love with you
And wouldn't want to doubt my heart.

You say my heart may not exist.
I know it does but isn't what
I once believed. This adds a twist
The like of which can save a plot.

Feelings and thoughts are kept apart
Unfairly by the words we choose.
Find me a better name than heart
By which to call the mind I lose.

Sophie Hannah

Courtship Dance

Your man plays cool, your man plays safe
But couldn't you like an acrobat, a tightrope-walking wife?

Your man wouldn't know, but don't you ever go
For the disreputable charmer or the milk-white dairy-farmer?

Your man will never go, but couldn't you, even so,
Fall for a wheeler-dealer or a two-hand reeler?

You're fine, you're Belfast 9, but why shouldn't you
Go west go south go sip at the mouth of the wild child-stealer?

Carol Rumens

Raw

He did not understand her rage.
Food was short and he had contacts,
had butchered well during the war,
the colonel still asked for his best cuts,
housewives on points queued for his sausages,
begged for mince under the counter,

      but shut in his cold room
he sliced and jointed, cleaving lambs
from neck to crotch, his heart bleeding,
and he posted her yielding parcels
in leaking greaseproof of kidney, top rump,
plump breasts, which the postman left
by the back entry

   till one hot Thursday after closing
he crept round, slipped through her letter box
slices of liver thick and damp, and waited
as summoned by the clatter she stood rigid
at the red lipped succulence wetting her toes.

Janet Fisher

Frida Kahlo Answers Shakespeare's Letters

Tragedy is the most ridiculous thing - Frida Kahlo

Little cry-baby, you know I adore you.
My painted kiss on your brow has opened
a red-rimmed eye that talks.
But those bastards, they only listen to scandal.

What can they say against us? I'm eighteen
here, in a suit and waistcoat. Handsome? Yes,
and still pretty in skirts.
I'll always have a boy's silky moustache.

Who can kiss it away? None of your bloody
tyrants, time or men or women. Look how the moon
meets the sun in my skies.
Old fat-cheek sun. Fattened on our blood.

We're all suns, nursing at one another's fucking
hearts like infants, till you'd think they'd
dry hard and clack together.
But not yours or mine. They fill again, fresh.

Look at me here, with one of my monkeys. Damn
him, he hangs on! He's jealous. He'll bite.
I've done the black wires
of my hair, and each tear, with a sharp brush.

And here, me in a steel bosom, banged up
for my son-of-a-bitch spine. If it weren't
rotten, darling, I'd fly.
No, but I'm yours, Will, my bald sweetheart.

You'll be my sugar skull, this Day of the Dead,
bald even of flesh.

Rosemary Norman

Friday Night

Wait
It is waiting and stillness
That is the heart of the matter
Waiting on the edge of sound
Waiting forever for a voice
For the movement
That is no parlour trick
For the air to part
The stillness to erupt
Into danger   excitement
That races the concealed heart
That beats it faster
Than love or sex

Waiting
It is waiting and stillness
Listening through the boredom
Listening through the noise
Through thought
Distraction   diversion
Straining to hear beyond number

It is waiting and stillness
Some try counting
Some discipline
Some pain
Some are reined like horses
Some take the stillness to them
Like a lake and wait knowing
Some may achieve silence

Wait
We must wait
The door opens gradually
The Sabbath Bride walks slow
Weighed heavy with jewels

Berta   Freistadt

52

Bathsheba at the River

After making love to Bathsheba and on hearing of her pregnancy, David,
knowing that Uriah will realize it is not his own child his wife is bearing,
sends him to certain death at the front line of battle. The baby dies, as God's
punishment to David.

Sun glances off the water.
Wading in up to my thighs
I break its silver
— shimmer my breasts taut with it;
my sucked-in feel-the-cold belly.

The river
beds my weight
in its sleek pebbles.
I can smell the mud bank
its green-ness of fronds.

A hawk scuds the sky,
hovers.
The trees thrill and filter.
I slide in through their song.

You will not see me now
from your roof top.
Criss-crossed with leaves.
Camouflaged with driftwood.

Our invisible child
latched to my nipple
pulls at the brown circle
unable to feed from its
full pitcher.

Now we float.
Grow less fretful.
The water nurses us.
Long and low
you must call
if you must call.

I hear my name
at the mouth
of the river
—listen for definition
through death to
two parts; a husband,
a child
move between us
on your couch.

Each time you
dip into me
with royal appetite
you enter
two ghosts—
grief. Absence.

Long and low
you must call.

I may
or may not
come
dripping, puckered
to the palace.

Linda Rose Parkes

That War

My plan was, admittedly, vague:
to walk on the tracks and roads of the garrigue
in the general direction of Masmolène-
la-Capelle. And — no, it was not that clever
to come without maps. We came upon it, however,
by instinct. Or rather, having resigned ourselves
to walk for the fun of it, past the olive groves,
the vines, the stubble fields, the fields of stones,
we suddenly saw — *I* saw — a village loom
beyond an 'Impasse' sign. We trundled down
the last impassable slope. We could ascertain
the name, only by walking along the road
to the crossed-through exit sign of the village: Masmolène.

So a truce, on aims and methods. We agreed
to strike uphill for the chapel, end derision
of female orienteering, male precision.
Mean of you, after that try for togetherness,
to launch from the ramparts a great arc of piss
on arrival. When we got back, I wrote this.

Penny McCarthy

55

A Dream of Fair Men

I am head of a Banana Republic
but we are having a military *coup*.
I run to my palace. Gunshot.
The General is there in confused occupancy.
I learn that I am to be his prize.

'OK, OK, I will go to that room with you.'
(He has greasy red hair: I quite like him)
'But I'll have to pick up a few things first.
Stay there.' I drift around the corridors
chatting to my staff, who do not seem aware

that power has changed hands. When I return,
he is awaiting me on a dirty palette. Most appealing.
I lift off my nightdress and lie by him
but we have absolutely no privacy. People enter
or leave the room, talking to us. He tells me

that he loves me, and he will give me a child.
I am flattered but my childbearing days
are over. He is unperturbed. He takes from his pocket
a substantial slab of chocolate. We eat.
Because this is only a *coup*, after all,

not a revolution. A revolution is not a dinner party.

Julia Casterton

Immortality

On the eve of my thirtieth birthday,
I dreamt that my mother hired my assassin.
I ran, but he caught up with me
just as I was about to board a boat.
He pushed me against a rail
the way a man does in a pubescent fantasy.
'Look there,' he said, pointing to the sun.
Cold metal pressed against my temple.
The shot imploded in my head.
Again, again, again, thirty times he shot
and each shot said, 'Dead dead dead'.

How evil of them, I thought,
Once would've done the trick.
Finally, quiet.
I straightened up and turned,
slowly. A smile played about my lips.
He dropped the gun in awe.
I kicked it overboard with just one flick
of my ankle, the way I once saw Lauren Bacall
do it. 'Alright,' I said. 'Alright.
Let's talk reasonably about this now.
You got a light?'

Cate Parish

Choices

Her white hands
burrow through atta, she calls brown flour,
and he adds pani laughing and she
says water, he namak and adds the salt.

Her gold thread sari border shines like
her newly wedded laughter,
he taught her recipes and words and threw
Indian customs across oceans and floors, she
learnt to bow her head
and raise it only for Angrezi parties.

Some of her children slipped from her, clotted
blood sliding
between her legs and
girl children flowed like monsoon rain until a
boychild she
thought she'd delivered happiness but
nothing changed.

Her kheema learns to fly,
she scrubs
the stubborn haldi from the walls, it smiles
yellow like
the August sun on her wedding day.

Maya Chowdhry

Steeplechase Park

after a painting by Reginald Marsh

In Steeplechase Park
We ride and we swing,
We light up in the dark,
We forget all our pain
In the lift and the flight:
Everything's thrilling,
Everything's right.

We roll onto our backs,
Our skirts billow high,
Our legs open slightly,
There's a look in our eye
Alluring the riders
Who smile at us hard
Before they divide us.

In Steeplechase Park
A man tries to mount
The mare of his choice
And finds that he can't.
He wallops her rump,
Then has her shot,
Says the filly won't jump.

Frances Nagle

A Lover's Promise

I will be there for you
behind the unwanted voices
on your answer-phone,
in each envelope
with its unknown writing,
in each long grey moment
you spend on your back, chasing sleep.

I will be there
in each little red car
that draws up behind you
the driver a shadowed shape
in your rear-view mirror
applying bright pink lipstick
to a pout you still long to kiss.

I will never leave you.
I will be the mask
on the face of the woman
you are trying to make love to;
I will widen the grin she wears
as you clamp your lips down
on hers, silencing a scream.

Sue Rose

Angel Wrestling

Angel Wrestling

Angel threw me naked across his shoulder
and gallopped round the flat in full view
of the spilling pub across the road.
When I shut myself in the bathroom
Angel picked up the hall entryphone
and said *OK, OK, I'll tell her. No problem*

then barged in and yelled *The landlord
thinks you should behave.* Angel almost
broke my neck between his legs, rigid
with arched back pleasure. *If you hear a click
just carry me to hospital* I whispered.
It'll be quadroplegia. I will, said Angel
if they'll put us in the same bed.

Angel spat wine and water over me
rubbed a broken peach down my spine
then swallowed. He kept me in his belly
three days and threw me up at Nineveh,
expecting me to do the business. Which I did,
knowing by then that angels need respect
as well as wrestling. As do whales.

Julia Casterton

Houdini

It is not clear how he entered me
or why he always has to escape.
Maybe he's just proving to the crowds
he can still do it — He whispers
half-words which bloom in the dark
Ma ha ma ha.

Sometimes he feeds me cough medicine.
Or bathes his genitals in salt water.
Then heaves his body upwards
as if pressing against a lid.
At least he prefers me
to his underwater box, to the manacles
which clank on his moon-white skin.
I wonder what it is exactly
he sees within me?
He touches my insides as though
he'd sighted the first landplants —
I'm catching cloud between my fingers.

Tonight the wind whips through my stomach
over knots of trees and sharp rocks.
When he rushes out of me the crowd gasps —
and I implode from sheer emptiness.

Moniza Alvi

Own Home

I was born into Hell.
In May the central heating's still on as well as
the Cosy Glo, and while
they watch the snooker they dip into assortments

of Fancy Cakes.
Upstairs the lilac nylon velour of Hell's surfaces sucks
you under; Hell's lilac
air is perfumed to drug you into being pleasant.

On nested tables,
each one smaller and more pointless than its superior,
lie war albums,
tiny brass war memorials, brass howitzers, tiny helmets.

The roar is Hell's
planes taking off and landing all day and most of the night
and the hiss
is of rapists in tight collars overtaking on the motorway.

Children return
in striped ties from private schools to gravel, to Cosy Glos
to en suite,
festooned, four-bedroomed car ports, to their only homes,

in Hell. Limbo is
to lie under the chaotic drugged smile of Queen Anne's Lace
under the one tree
in the private field small as an executive's lounge.

Judy Gahagan

Potato City

For Kevin and Maisie

Her name was Beryl.
Like the precious stone.
Bald and louche,
her job was beating children
and stuffing them in cots
that didn't fit
or stuffing chickens
down their hopeless throats.
Some of them were more than twice her size
so discipline was obviously
essential.
And discipline in fact
was her strong point.
Her pigeon-chested chest
was rigid with it.

Her colleague was a Miss
Kartoffel-Salat —
a sullen creature
Uncle P. produced
(judging by the idiotic name).
Bored? Was that it?
Bored to tears like me?
We should have gone to that
Potato City, alluded to
in your more garrulous moments,
where people with big heads
wear hats on spikes
they sink into their skulls
in special rituals
involving brewing the resulting discharge.

The atmosphere
begins to get oppressive,
and non-potatoes feel like creeping out.
In or out or up or down — who cares?

In the thumping subterranean darkness,
hot potato breasts,
potato knees,
potato knuckles
and potato cheeks
focus singlemindedly
on merry-making.
Even in the nurseries
lunar babies
butt each other with their heads
and laugh.

Selima Hill

The 'No' Madonnas

For the one
who said yes,
how many
said no?

Of course,
there was
the Sumatran who refused
and then the Nubian,
then the Swede,
who shied away
from bearing the Word,
though the chance
was offered ...
a Finn, a Chinese ...
Declining politely
they carried on
with the dusting
or with its equivalent
so the question
was left
to an Indian, a Lapp,
who were questioned by God

for outrageous assent,
for in sweetest closeness
all being is rent.

But those who said no
for ever knew
they were damned
to the daily
as they'd disallowed
reality's madness,
its astonishment.

So the moment passed
and the fissure closed,
an angel withdrew,
no message sent,
and the lady prepared
her adequate meal
—food of free will—
from which God
a while longer
was absent.

Gwyneth Lewis

Red Mist

You could wear different shoes,
Lose all the worthwhile things you have to lose;

You could go mad and howl
From a high tree through darkness, like an owl —

No part of me would change
However sick you were, however strange.

Your future, near and distant,
Is safe, as long as I remain consistent.

If, one day, you commit
A crime, I'll burn all evidence of it.

When it arrives, my doom
Will be a red mist entering the room.

Sophie Hannah

Dancing

Nothing has dulled my feel for earth,
its stern gravity-pull,
its cushion of dark.

Neighbours in the flat below
hear my feet tapping on carpet
while the rest of the house sleeps.
When I dance in daylight, boards creak again
with the samba, the tango, the waltz.

I have acres and acres to dance through,
recharging as I go. Sometimes I find
a partner in a shopping-mall,
or in an uncut field,
my party-face sparking till I'm giddy.

I whirl past tiredness, changing the beat,
everything spinning —
I am flying at last...

My eyes glisten, past bitterness,
I dance in my sleep.
Whole streets fly by me —
whole streets have started dancing.

Katherine Gallagher

Eisriesenwelt

Eisriesenwelt — the Ice Giants' World, is the largest ice-cave in the world, high in the Austrian Alps. It is full of ice-formations such as the Icewall and the Icedoor.

In the world of the ice giants
I'm not afraid.

Today, I glided into the cave.
I wore glass shoes.

When I held my hand
against the light

I could see the veins
tunnelling through my palm

like a system of caves.
I stripped,

so the ice could fill me.

    *

When I left home
I sculpted my parents in ice
but they kept melting.
The tutors complained.
They said water was formless.
I needed a fridge large as Eisriesenwelt,
26 miles long, to store my art.

So I tried glass.
Sometimes I touch the ice
and think it's fire —
the white heat of the kiln
where glass sculptures are cast.
I tried to rebuild my grandmother's greenhouse.

I made glass trees, glass rain, and a glass grandmother,
but they annealed too fast. They cracked.

★

Welcome to my studio
full of figures and towers.
Some of the towers are people.
Some of the people are towers.

Don't blame the artist.
I make what the ice-giants dictate.
If they say stay in the studio overnight,
I stay.

They made me carve
a stone dress for my mother.
I am not to blame
for its weight.

I was the lacemaker
who used frost
instead of silk
for her underclothes.

★

I created an entire wardrobe —

a dress of green ice
for my mother the sea,

a dress of blue ice
for my mother the sky,

a dress of black ice
for my mother the earth.

Her body shone through the green dress
like a reef.

Her body shone through the blue dress
like the sun.

Her body shone through the black dress
like a corpse.

My hands were raw from sewing
molten gossamers of spun glass

which shattered
when worn.

She was a tower of broken windows.

      ★

My mother has put all her clothes on,
armouring herself against me.
If I ask the right question
one of the dresses will answer.
They speak different languages.
There is the language of glass
window-glass and lead-crystal,
and the language of ice —
blue, green and black ice.

She leads me to a house
where I spend five years
surrounded by emerald and ruby tears,
by turquoise and sapphire tears.
She has shed so many jewels
they form seas in our rooms.
I call my mother's seas
Sea of Sadness, the Bitter Sea,
Sea of Madness, the Guilty Sea.

      ★

Welcome to our sitting-room.
It's hard to cross it, so we don't.

We're those two
facing each other across the ice.

The walls are furred.
My mother is waiting for me to defrost them.

Long blue icicles hang from the ceiling
like rain from a permanent storm.

Even in caves, the wind can blow out light.
The draught has plunged us into darkness.

My mother's tears freeze. They fall
onto her body like stitches in a glass dress

knitted from the seas of her sadness.
Dresses within dresses. Mothers within daughters.

Because I am young. Because I am alive,
the Icedoor is open. I remember

we passed it before the fridge took over.
Perhaps on a postcard, in a letter.

It was a mouth. My mouth.
I said yes. I'll visit. Every weekend.

Yes. I'll come back, defrosting,
cleaning the scraps from the shelves.

Mow the lawn. Mow the mountains of Austria.

I got up. I slipped. I crawled along the floor.
Down frozen waterfalls I slid. Down the Icewall.

The cable-car was waiting for me.

The inn was warm. My life was warm.

Pascale Petit

Gravity

Teeth

This is X who has all her own teeth.
Her mother is horrified by this.

Look into her mouth. She still has them.
perfect pearls. Milk stones. Pure ivory.

Not a filling, no receding gums.
X was a woman with a lively

smile. Since she was a girl. No dark holes.
her mother wore, still does, false teeth. Tusks,

badly fitted, left something unsaid
— a tiny gap between tooth and gum.

Her mum's teeth, in a glass tumbler, swam
at night: a shark's grin; a wolf's slow smirk.

What upsets her mother now, oddly,
is this: X had such beautiful lips.

This morning the men broke in — 8 AM.
X was wearing her dressing gown, white

towelling. They came wearing her number
on their arms. **Did you know,** her mother says,

**they taped my daughter's mouth to choke her
screams. They covered her mouth in white tape.**

The small boy pulled at the sharp trousers.
He was soundless. The big men flung him

into that grey corner. His voice burst.
He will stand there, that height, forever, see

those minutes grab and snatch and repeat
themselves. The men in plain clothes have claws;

they attack his mother like dogs, gagging her,
binding her, changing her into someone

else. He will watch her hands smash and thrash.
His hands making a church, then a tall

steeple. He crosses his fingers. Squeezes them.
His hands wet themselves. He is five years old.

He knows his address. He knows his name.
He has ten fingers. He counts them again.

This is X who has all her own teeth.
Came to this country with her own teeth.

Soundbites will follow. Lies will roll
tomorrow. The man with the abscess

will say she had a weak heart. High blood.
Illegal. Only doing his job.

Fill it in. Write it down. Bridge the gap.
Give him a stamp of approval: silver

or gold or NHS, she resisted arrest;
there's your cause of death. On a plate.

She was wrong. Give her a number. Think
of a number. Take away the son.

Jackie Kay

77

Obsessive Compulsive Disorder

It comes on slowly
the doubting illness
checking, checking
checkerboard, stepping

first in the dark, then the light
off, on,
the gas, the water.

Outside the rooster is crowing
and leaves will fly back to the wrong
side of the railway track.
They do things like that.

As if the appletree
could fast when it rains,
the winter stop short,
indoors there are rituals
against loss, against change.
So much has been taken from you
the horse already bolted

but there is always more
to be taken — blown across the yard
like chickenfeed, seed, cloud,
an empty stable blurred
behind the windy
flowershow.

Stare at the oven,
the lights, the taps,
the cooker. Count to thirty.
Are there stirrings?
Off, off, off, off.

Turn away, turn back,
peer into the stable.
Those cracks of light

are pond, lake, afternoon,
the horse gone.
Read the hay dark, doubting.

                                    Jane Duran

Christmas Presents

Christmas, very, have a merry very
A very merry Christmas, trilled the cards.
In gynae wards that means: There is a future.

I lay there, while you sorted friends and stamps.
The local wise man had come up with gold:
A benign cluster. You'll be home by Christmas.

Nothing to say. When I was tired, we held hands.

But next bed's visitors were staring.
Why us? The colour of our hair, perhaps?

You didn't notice, so I didn't tell you.

Next day (another day!) her bed was stripped.

Her lovers (husband? daughter?) hadn't cared
To watch death creeping up and down her face;
Stared at us out of tact, no doubt,
Somewhere to rest their smarting eyes, but also
(I like to think) because we were,
Of all things, human;

Human, of all things.

                            U.A. Fanthorpe

The Lewis Chessmen

British Museum; Scandinavian, c. 1150

These people have known nothing beside warfare —
eyes strained against ambush, fists clamped fast
on spear or sword. Even the bishops, giving the world
their two benedictional fingers, plainly belong
to the Church Militant. They proclaim
God's judgement on the foe, the obdurate Others.

The king's gifts to his thanes are mailshirt and spear,
helmet and hard-edged sword. A handful champ their shields:
berserkers, frantic to surrender
to the wonderful extravagance of rage.
Most, though, face out doom
with dour mouths, driven purely by a formal pattern
they cannot move beyond. 'Better a man should die
than live a life of blame.' The sombre queens
will offer their ale-horns only to heroes.

I was a child when I saw them first.
The shock of that mass glare still works in me.
And the instant after, staring eyeball to eyeball, sensing
their stubborn resistance, their grief;
saluting, below all reason, unlooked-for, the presence of kin.

Gillian Spraggs

I'm Flying Over America for the First Time at 55

Piggy back on the massive balloon
of sky. Up up up, faded blue silks
straining seams that leak sunlight.

Our little silver cigar basket
bumps on cloud, buzzes as if
it could point its nose and go;
as if it wasn't fastened invisibly
with guy ropes to the achingly blue
panels of our vast convoy of air.
A cloud moves its massive shoulder;
we buck and judder on our tether.

Space opens; a fly, looking down
the velvet shute of a flower's throat,
we see the scattered pollen of haycocks,
and tender purple twisted river veins.
Land; its texture a lover's skin,
every wrinkle and fold speaking intimacy.

A mile in the air, swinging
from the wrists of the sky,
my own heart is lit, swollen
as a pumpkin over that old body.

Soft lavender varicosities,
little rivers, run together
pluming their fluids into the sea.
Tiny boats, each wearing
a white lamb-chop frill,
skitter on our restless shadow,
as clouds turn over.

Setting out is forgotten;
arrival is irrelevant;
only going matters
ravished by a traveller's
pain, that perpetual goodbye
of always seeing better as you go.

Kate Foley

Soul-Searching

She was built like a fisherman
and wore gumboots for the job.
Handled her tools so roughly I thought.
Anyway, I wasn't there to nit-pick
but it narked me how she prised
the sawn chest-cavity open
and slapped the organs out
in handfuls on the marble.
'Offal, isn't it?' she said, grinning,
her captive audience greening (medical students —
first years, I think they were).

Then, slicing up the bit that was the heart,
grumpy as a cheese counter attendant poking
and probing into what could have been
clandestine love affairs for all she knew,
she mumbled up her sleeve, 'No sign of
Mitral Valve Disease as previously suspected'.

Not that I was there to judge you understand...
But even though the brain was like moulded mushroom pâté,
I don't think she should have
tipped the skull back quite like that —
much as she was emptying a bin.

I can't think why it was wrong though.
I'm not one for a lot of fuss myself —
not one for a show, but I did keep thinking,
If his mother could see him now...
Pale gold his hair was, his skin, potato-white,
— except for the black tattoos like potato eyes,
and his groin, the bits — you know —
well she hadn't covered them up.
With his face folded over like that,
it might have seemed a bit silly I suppose,

and with his brain in a bucket....

Marita Maddah

82

Gravity

What do the men in helmets think
striding past me with their sealed packages?

Do they see a woman with dust in her hair
hovering at a door which doesn't say 'Psychotherapist'
though everyone in the building must know?
Battersea Business Centre, thin corridors
where the air drains me of breath.
I can slip away, I don't have to be here.

They tread past, steaming slightly in their black bike gear
absorbed in the work of the world
vizors jacked up, chin guards jutting.
A nose like a drugged laboratory animal
exposed.
Eyes counting, looking for room numbers.

I don't want her to open the door.
The soft blonde smile that opens to chaos
a blur of plants, white threads drifting from the cushions
and behind my eyes, the shredding.

Stay with the work of the world.

The men's boots are so big, clumpy
— space boots, giants' clogs, a child in his father's shoes —
as if they feared loss of gravity
weightlessness.

Caroline Natzler

Mother, Mother

What have you done with my friends and my loves
     Mother, Mother?
What have you done with my friends and my loves
     That were so dear to me oh?
They just weren't good enough for you, my dear
     Stay close to me my darling.

Where's my share of a woman's skills
     Mother, Mother?
Where's my share of a woman's skills?
     I've looked for it everywhere.
Drowned in my soups and baked in my cakes
     Daughter, daughter
I skewered and sewed them tight.

What have you done with my lovely body
     Mother, Mother?
What have you done with my lovely body
     My right to love and be loved?
It should be me that goes to the ball
     Daughter, daughter,
It should be me that goes to the ball.
     Don't even think of it, darling.

What have you done with my father dear
     Mother, Mother?
What have you done with my father dear
     That was my other heart?
You dared, you two, betray me so,
     Daughter, daughter,
Be proud of him, love him now, if you dare
     My heel goes through his cheek.

Harriet Proudfoot

Cut

I've nicked a neck or two
in my time
almost cut off the ears
of old dears
all tight permed in bingo blue.
I've razored and feathered
with amazing skill
cut bobs for fat slobs
Watch me!
I am an expert. I'm sharp
I've scrunched and crimped
given body to the limp
added volume
bleached out grey
dyed nearly every day.
I've scissored my way
to a hell of varicose veins
and tint stains
that won't wash away.

One fine day
I'll crack
go mad
and cut up rough.

Joyce Goldstein

85

Wall of Death

He settles his leather crotch
carefully on the saddle;
eases his wrist down
the tight funnel of his wet-suit black.
Chains dazzle from boot
and shoulder; gold
winks from his thatched chest.

She is all pink; accessory
to the pink flashes on the monster
fat black bike.

Hup! She's in the saddle
nestling in the template
of his back and thigh.

In synchrony they put on
their great round helmets,
each slip of a face eclipsed.

He stamps his foot.
Obediently the bike roars;
then like a maddened tiger
hurls them up the wall.

Hanging over the lip
of the amphitheatre
our faces flinch, moon pale.

Now they are scythes,
flashing round
the waist of the wall.

Up! the bike flings them
to the brim of our faces.

Angles resolve.
She is unfolding.

She is upright
on the flattened bike.
Our breath stops.
She stands on the saddle's edge,
tensile, poised as a pendulum
plumb down from the sky.
He is a blob of solder.
He sticks her to the hot machine.

Graceful as the slow infolding
of a night flower she sinks
unhurried to the cantle.
She waves. We roar.
We are inside the body of an angry bull.

With a twitch of pink nylon
she says no to death,
not today, and a cool
hand kindly scratches our poll;
blood and circuses dim
as the mad bike pants
to a dumb standstill;
its sweat-glossed hide fades
to dead metal as we shuffle out.

Kate Foley

the seamstress

she looks up
the needle swaying
under the weight of the words
red thread scratching the
outer seams of a silk kameez

she can't recognise your
almond eyes dripping onto the cloth
your body has changed
become distorted
your tawny skin seems
different because it has lain
under a woman's hand

she thinks luckily she's
already measured your
breasts, your hips, your
inside leg because now
she doesn't want to put
her tape measured hand there

it's no longer
a woman's inside thigh
the measurement has
expanded
become an unknown domain
a terrifying territory

and now your clothes
are one size larger
the cloth hanging wide around
your breasts
your inside thigh
and your salwaar so
tight around your ankle
you can hardly get them on.

Maya Chowdhry

Burnt Notebook

Burnt Notebook

The title of this poem belongs to Anna Akhmatova, who had reason to mean it literally.

i

I should write this in code,
or the private language of the Japanese court women:
how, a small speechless child, I feared the touch

of her freckled competent hands,
how I hid from them

deep on the riverbed, below the green
unbroken surface: and even in that cool

silence,   the current pulling
like weights in the hem of my sleeves, the clamour

her fingers made in my sex   still floated down
and rang through my arms and legs like the long boom
in a bell tower   and scarred rings on the water

ii

Invisible behind glass
I watch the children

out on the street
taking turns with the bicycle

and the Sainsbury's trolley,
arguing, comforting

the smallest boy
who totters with open arms

into the noise.
The wide street shelters them,

while I on the second floor
a secret woman,

knowing what fingers can do
with small bodies,

I keep myself here
behind glass

not to be two again,

nor her
ever

iii

This notebook
I will put on the fire

coming downstairs
in the dark   and levering

the round grey lid
off the coke boiler —

rank breath of anthracite,
scant glow, ash.

I drop the notebook
flat on the embers

muffle the clattering lid,
climb the stairs, leaving

pink covers
curling like ribbon

scrawled pages,
linen scorching;

and will the fire
free me   by breakfast time

or will there be words
bright on the coals:

'her hands'
perhaps, or 'fear'

the evidence
I char to forgetfulness,

she always wanted

iv

Come stand by my desk
keep her away from these words

or let the musicians from
the corners of my room loop up

the barbed wire of their chords
let Beethoven

enclose the room with his pain
abandon her

there on the stairs   leaning
one hand against the wall

out of breath   smiling
as ever   the warm light

of the autumn evening
trapped in her silver hair

v

If she'd let me write

I could stand at the top of the stairs
and wait for her

If I had a pen
I could write myself courage

I'd say:

If I had a pen
and could write
the truth on paper

but she
is standing

blocking my narrow stairs

with her smile
her hands

vi

Every home should have one
sickly young girl, whose feet

tucked under the brown
rug on the sofa

are never seen
running downstairs, dancing:

Beth
in Little Women,   or that

Victorian heroine
cured

of wanting
having given

her body to the poor
who   blesses

the weeping tormentor,
dies —

Remember the blessing.
Every family needs

a child to absolve them
of their cruelty,

and vanish.
Now, every time

spread on the couch
in defiance and recollection

I wait for the man
who'll touch

the back of my throat
once   and make me

obedient at last
throw up my body.

Quick, the matches!
Burn up the page. Her surviving

relatives, glancing
at a book on an airport stall

might recognise..
Can't you see they're like her?

the firm step and the white
innocent hair, they'll send

the Special Branch
to my door

stop my writing hand with a bodybelt
tape up my mouth

and weep in the hospital
when the life support's turned off

and I'll have been
Beth again
for another generation

vii

Useless to burn the book
even   not write

she's everywhere. I'm
in the outdoor shower, the sun

pouring colour through the strung
beads of the water   a plane

goes over
and it's her

assessing the curve of my hip,
peering —

Or I'm waiting
for my lover to phone. That's her

laughter out in the street:
Who'd want

to see you anyway?   I'm
thirteen again,

95

sweating, with greasy hair
and ink-stained hands

writing to my one
moved-away friend

I seal up the letter
but she

can repeat every word,
jeering.

viii

All my life, those times
the ceiling draws in, I've heard
a doorbell ringing

and leaned out of windows, run down to the street
to find

in the shade of the porch, on the path by the lavender,
no-one. Has she come, my visitor

the woman who should have known, the one who wrote
her report to the court: I know there has been concern

to take me away at last   or is it her
long dead, her hair

silver under the streetlamp, carrying
a leather suitcase

tears in her eyes   that pleading
knifeblade voice:

Take me in.

                                    Ruth Valentine

Less and Less

Gossip

On the phone you told me
that the baby weighed heavy
in you: the lost baby, the dead

one, hers, a woman distraught
a woman not knowing who her child was
or where (the worst)

where he in dread of the dark
had gone (Somewhere terrible
she harboured and was sure of,

some chinkless limbo he crouched in
with his sad strange grave-goods
calling and calling for her)

And she, telling you this
so that she might not be mad,

so that your voice, not hers,
would twist like the cord
which throttled him

And now you pass the weight;
the mystery of all he might have said
or loved,

the thousand flowers of language
that waited for him. And later

I too must tell, all of us,
pass him from hand to hand,
make a nest, many,

weave light feathers, help
her to do this; dexterously
unwind the bad shroud,

swear to it: that some
are silenced but everywhere,
and some are nowhere, but

comfortably, and sing
like the wind sings

Alison Fell

Less and Less

Daylight hours when the house returns to me
I walk barefoot, alone, through all the rooms,
in cool possession, touching this, touching that,
releasing everything from vows and obligation,
abiding only in what's not in my keeping,
the blue green blue of sky, boughs, bay.

At night I pray the great battles inside you
will end, and with them, your sadness.
Who needs a golden dome, a vaulted ceiling?
Pain and all her grown-up children can worship anywhere.
My love, I promise. It will take less and less to console us.

Nadya Aisenberg

Say 'Moose' For Me

I want to pull you back to say 'moose' for me
with that double 'o' sound, each 'o' single, separate,
hanging perfect in the air like smoke rings
two 'o's suspended, soft in the back palate like an owl —
like that poem by Elizabeth Bishop: *A moose
has come out of the impenetrable wood.*

Things you didn't say to me
in your wry New England undertone,
move into my mind, hunching their shoulders.
I run back through time. I'll carry your books.
Let's both go paddling your canoe, I'll be in your camp,
we'll practise pissing though a tap. Talk to me.

You were pretty as the woodcutter's daughter
fresh as the third son out for his fortune
good day, good morrow, madam, sir, a feast,
a meeting in the forest.
You left me alone in a wood at night
where the trees gang up and mutter.

Your perfect absence, nothing else would do.
You drove off, a mad coachman beating the horse,
turning and grinning from between your sideburns.
And something else ran in front of my car, tiny feet
faster than clockwork: a mouse in the headlights,
desperate for shadows.

Christina Dunhill

Alice

You were attracted to fires; when you unearthed
a sapling and dragged it to our room
to consecrate the chimney, I held your hand
under the tap, kept the swelling down.
When your lit cigarettes fell under your feet
as you drove, in the passenger seat I put
them out. That van, last remnant of your dad's
hippie days, got us through Georgia, six hours
flat. The family was waiting for you to come

back to the fold, could see you were troubled,
that your body was soaked to the bone
with poison, had burst a vein clear across
your thigh. The doctors in Alabama could find
no cause, but the Lord had His reasons.
You thought it was from too many men, they'd
'rammed something loose'. Your mother
wouldn't let you take your sickbed until
you'd confessed your sins. The doctors said
your father had a couple months left. You sat
together in the kitchen, rolling cigarettes.

I miss you now, wonder if you still flirt games
of eight ball off marine cadets for drinks
in those bars with red lights and no windows.
All our songs are gone in the jukebox
at the Kettle, the photo of the girl we took
for dead over our usual booth has left
a fair patch in the wood where she'd hung.
Somewhere you burn your bridges with a blowtorch.

Tamar Yoseloff

At Your House

Arriving at your house, I saw
the azaleas were coming into bloom,
sounding out another spring
as you were, fighting every inch
of pain, marshalling
your body's slow flight —

— into escapades, trips still planned:
your diary full, you an eightyish
wanderer, mother of six, arranging
for them and beyond, your grandchildren,
a wedding, the first call...

I can scarcely bear to look
at the tidiness — your garden just so
as if you'd been working here all morning
among golden ash, prunus, white gums and rowans —

where flowers grew in your arthritic hands,
blossoms filling, where trees gave up their dark.

Katherine Gallagher

Prayer

has nothing of the grandeur
or the violence of crowds
but circles, stockinged
in its own quiet sphere

like lamplight sealing off what gloom sees
by its cone against the dark,
an interval when, weightless,

the body loses cut and thrust,
rises like a plume of smoke
to add its grievances to air's.

Prayer
is like watering the plants,
popping out to get the paper,
a trundling, a pottering,

an audience for dust
that settles even as the duster's hand
moves across the grain.

Prayer can interrupt itself — fling
instructions over shoulders, offer
what it saved you on the shelf;

resume itself, its murmuring,
like berries, herbs
left drying in the sun

as, moving out of earshot,
you find your own momentum,
your freedom not to pray.

Prayer is not a scourge.
Though the head bows, the back stoops,
it is a lifting, a soft and drifting
spiral like the echoes of a string plucked,

a sky to feel alone in,
how small one is, how packed
the earth with people

how far the neighbour's radio
— as skin meets stone —
recedes
and amber beads count amber suns
that are still to rise, still to set.

Prayer is what we all do,
surely,
when all else fails.

Mimi Khalvati

Houses of Letters

Eyes like dried up lakes
want rain torrents
floods great gushing
waves of sadness
to flow and fill
the hollow
orange to indigo
on the clouds horizon

words match feelings
in snatches
no sentences
no orderly lines
of prose or verse
only my skin speaks

I want to be there
I want to stay
in the sky forever
watching the sun

rise beyond
the silver strip
want words to
jump from envelopes
become arms around
a dying friend

flying into the
southern hemisphere
close to the night
crescent moon smiles
at southern star
reflecting on
a tip of wing
and Africa
beneath the haze

I watch her sleep
in fading light
shudder shallow breaths
catch rays of sun
in copper hair
touch face
slip past memories
prepare myself
to let her go
along with dreams
of two women
growing old
in houses
full of letters

Seni Seneviratne

While Shepherds Watched their Flocks

The Lord is my shepherd
I'll wait for you in heaven, I say
And you say don't get in that coffin yet,
you're too alive for that wooden darkness
And I say get these fucken tubes out
they're stranglin my mind

the quiet waters by

yea though I walk in death's dark vale
you comfort me with chocolate eclairs and if sugar
is so bad for my healing why they channelling
it in through my veins with their fine white tubes
I shall not want he makes me down to lie
beside you, on the red satin for Tuesdays,
cerise for Fridays, not any Fridays left
I stay awake
all night
cause I don't want to go
in my sleep and the nurse says staying awake isn't living
And me to walk doth make

You say, I walk past your room six times a week
cause I don't recognise it's you
cause I don't want to see you dissolve into
a sticky yellow smell between your breath and the door
Within the paths of righteousness
if you love me enough you wouldn't be able to surrender

And my cup overflows.
And my cup overflows.

My table thou hast furnished in presence of my foes
and the doctor
comes in and says take a pill
for your plague, a placebo
for your straining Black psyche
My soul he doth restore again
Nothin' will bring you back to me, you say,

the whole of you, not that sloppy bit of flesh
hovering on the crisp hospital white sheets
like the starch would tear your skin
Goodness and mercy all my life
shall surely follow me

If I hadn't followed, if I had listened, if there wasn't
any doubt in my mind, if you had, if we had.
And in God's house for ever more
it was too late to live
with you, have kids with you, go on a round
the world cruise, do charity work, develop a dancer's body, eat
health food, dye my hair blue.
My head thou dost with oil anoint

My dwelling place shall be
My dwelling place
shall be
I can't live without you

In pastures green he leadeth me
And you say lets fuck before you
die, jus once and you think it's funny,
I can't get past the tubes let alone come,
it isn't no joke you slimy bastard
my last breath isn't a fucken last supper painting

You ask what is all this shit, you didn't go to
no convent school,
it was a dirty slum comprehensive
like a 60's window and concrete ship

You slap my arm and the drip yanks
out and my blood spurts on your face
and I start laughing and coughing blood
and it washes off
your skin but not your 'Queer Nation' t-shirt
and I say fuck you
the quiet waters by.

Maya Chowdry

Pieta (2)

death has scooped you
out of me
broken the cradle
of your arms
exiled you to the abominable
mantelpiece of candlesticks

I have a high room
filled with fury
where the fridge
ticks endlessly

neighbours rattle at the door
like dry beans
I take nothing from anyone

when I shut my eyes
I am totally invisible
only death can see me

tangled like a black goat
in the thicket of sheets

if I cannot have you
no one else will do

I will drool like an idiot
eat figs and ashes

stuff death
into my mouth
and suck it like a thumb

Alison Fell

Biographical notes

NADYA AISENBERG is a Visiting Scholar at Brandeis University, Massachusetts. She has published four books of non-fiction including *Ordinary Heroines: Transforming the Male Myth* in June 1994. She is the author of three books of poetry, most recently *Before We Were Strangers* (Forest Books, 1989).

MONIZA ALVI is one of the 1994 New Generation poets. Her collection *The Country at My Shoulder* (Oxford, 1993) was shortlisted for the Whitbread and the T.S. Eliot Prizes. She was joint winner of the Poetry Business competition, 1991, with Peter Daniels. She lives and teaches in South London.

JULIA CASTERTON wrote *Creative Writing - A Practical Guide* (Macmillan, 1986), *That Slut Cleopatra* (Turret Books, 1988) and *Troublesome Cattle* (with Liz Cashdan, Smith/Doorstop 1990). She helps edit *Ambit,* works for the City Lit and the Open University, and is bringing up her two daughters in London.

MAYA CHOWDHRY is also a film-maker, live artist and radio playwright. She wrote *The Heart and Heaven* (BBC Radio). Her poetry is collected in *Putting in the Pickle* and she has poems in *The Popular Front of Contemporary Poetry, Crazy Jig* and other anthologies.

CAROL ANN DUFFY was born in Glasgow in 1955. She has published four collections of poetry for Anvil: *Standing Female Nude* (1985), *Selling Manhattan* (1987), *The Other Country* (1990) and *Mean Time* (1993) which won both the Forward and the Whitbread Prizes. She lives in London and works as a freelance writer.

CHRISTINA DUNHILL (Editor) was shortlisted for the Arvon Prize, 1993. She also won prizes in the Bridport competition 1993 and The Kitley Trust 1994. She has been published in various magazines and the last two Oscars anthologies and is working on a first collection. She teaches creative writing in London.

JANE DURAN was born in Cuba in 1944, brought up in the US, and has lived in England since 1966. A pamphlet of her poems *Boogie Woogie* was published by Hearing Eye in 1991, a selection of her work in *Poetry Introduction 8* by Faber, 1993 and her first collection will be coming from Enitharmon in 1995.

U.A. FANTHORPE was born in Kent and lives in Gloucestershire. She taught for 16 years, dropped out and became a clerk. She has published five poetry collections with Peterloo Poets and her *Selected Poems* was published as a King Penguin in 1986. In 1994 she was nominated for Oxford Professor of Poetry.

ALISON FELL is a Scottish poet and novelist who lives and works in London. Her *Kisses for Mayakovsky* (Virago, 1984) won the Alice Hunt Bartlett Award for a first poetry collection. Her fifth novel, *The Pillow Boy of the Lady Onogoro* (Serpent's Tail, 1994) is a work of literary eroticism.

JANET FISHER is co-director of The Poetry Business in Huddersfield, co-editing *The North* magazine and Smith/Doorstop Books. She has had three pamphlets published and her work was represented in *New Women Poets* (Bloodaxe 1990).

KATE FOLEY was born in London in 1938. She left convent school with few qualifications but has always read and written poetry. She has been a midwife, teacher and conservator and now manages a team of heritage scientists. Her first collection *Soft Engineering* will be published by Onlywomen Press in 1994.

BERTA FREISTADT is a Londoner. Her first poem about furry animals was published in *The Observer* in 1948. With some work on style and content, she has since been published in several anthologies. She has taught women writing for nearly a decade and is alternately depressed and awed by their talent and commitment.

JUDY GAHAGAN left academic psychology for an intense relationship with poetry and fiction - and to develop the art of living between the cracks like a lizard. She has been published in most of the major poetry magazines, has three grown daughters and spends some of each year working in Italy.

KATHARINE GALLAGHER is an Australian poet resident in London since 1979. She has been published widely in the UK and Australia. Her most recent collections are *Finding the Prince* (Hearing Eye, 1993) and her translations of Jean Jacques Celly: *The Sleepwalker with Eyes of Clay* (Forest, 1994).

CHRISSIE GITTINS has worked as a writer-in-residence on an inter-generation project, in a hospice and in a prison. She is currently working on a seven schools poetry project in Buckinghamshire. Her work has been published in magazines and anthologies and her feature *Poles Apart* broadcast on Radio 4.

JOYCE GOLDSTEIN started working life as a librarian and went on to specialise in business information. She worked for over ten years as a researcher here and in the US. She has studied counselling and psychology and devotes as much time as possible to writing poetry and short stories.

EMMA GREENGRASS was born in 1967 and grew up in Clacton-on-Sea with fond memories of white stilettos and jumble sales. She now lives in the East End with her bicycle, writing poetry and stories and doing her secretary impression. She was runner-up for the Margot Jane Memorial Prize (Onlywomen Press) in 1993.

SOPHIE HANNAH is 23 and lives in Mancheser. She has published two collections of poetry: *Early Bird Blues* (Smith/Doorstop, 1993) and *Second Helping of Your Heart* (The Frogmore Press, 1994).

ROSANNA HIBBERT. The 'Institute' in my poem is the City Lit in London, to several of whose teachers I owe a great deal. I wrote for advertising and television for over 30 years: it was good, in my late fifties, to be free to start something new.

SELIMA HILL was born in London in 1945. She lives and works in Dorset with her artist husband and three children. She won First Prize in the Arvon/Observer Competition in 1989. She has published three collections with Chatto and two with Bloodaxe: most recently, *Trembling Hearts in the Bodies of Dogs* (1994).

MARIA JASTRZEBSKA was born in Warsaw and came to England as a child. She is author of *Postcards from Poland and Other Correspondences* with artist Jola Scicinska (Working Press). Her work appears in various anthologies including *Mustn't Grumble - Writing by Disabled Women*, (Womens Press, 1994) ed Lois Keith.

JACKIE KAY was born in 1961 and brought up in Scotland. Her first collection *The Adoption Papers* (Bloodaxe, 1991) won four awards. Her first collection for children *Two's Company* (Blackie, 1992) won the Signal Award 1993. Her second collection for adults is *Other Lovers* (Bloodaxe, 1994).

MIMI KHALVATI was born in Tehran in 1944. She has been widely published, including in *Sixty Women Poets* (Bloodaxe, 1993) and *The Forward Book of Poetry* (1993). She has two